BEYOND OUR DIMENSIONAL UNDERSTANDING

What Do We Really Know About Life and Total Reality

Ray Weaver Sr.

WESTBOW
P R E S S®
A DIVISION OF THOMAS NELSON
& ZONDERVAN

Scripture quotations marked (NIV) are taken from the Holy Bible, New International Version®, NIV®. Copyright © 1973, 1978, 1984, 2011 by Biblica, Inc.™ Used by permission of Zondervan. All rights reserved worldwide. www. zondervan.com The "NIV" and "New International Version" are trademarks registered in the United States Patent and Trademark Office by Biblica, Inc.™

Scripture taken from the King James Version of the Bible.

Scripture quotations taken from the New American Standard Bible® (NASB), Copyright © 1960, 1962, 1963, 1968, 1971, 1972, 1973, 1975, 1977, 1995 by The Lockman Foundation Used by permission. www.Lockman.org

WestBow Press books may be ordered through booksellers or by contacting:

WestBow Press
A Division of Thomas Nelson & Zondervan
1663 Liberty Drive
Bloomington, IN 47403
www.westbowpress.com
1 (866) 928-1240

Because of the dynamic nature of the Internet, any web addresses or links contained in this book may have changed since publication and may no longer be valid. The views expressed in this work are solely those of the author and do not necessarily reflect the views of the publisher, and the publisher hereby disclaims any responsibility for them.

Any people depicted in stock imagery provided by Getty Images are models, and such images are being used for illustrative purposes only. Certain stock imagery © Getty Images.

ISBN: 978-1-9736-4783-6 (sc)
ISBN: 978-1-9736-4785-0 (hc)
ISBN: 978-1-9736-4784-3 (e)

Library of Congress Control Number: 2018914489

Print information available on the last page.

WestBow Press rev. date: 12/26/2018

I use the "The Holy Bible" (NIV, KJV or NAS versions of the bible for all Biblical Quotes), but many times only use excerpts from them or put them in my terms that fits the subject being discussed but does not deviate from scriptural meaning.

Ray Weaver Sr. Previous Books

"A Search for The Truth"

Published by WestBow Press a division of Thomas Nelson and Zondervan, Released in July 30, 2014

"Why Did God Create Us"

Published by WestBow Press a division of Thomas Nelson and Zondervan, Released in October 30, 2017

"The Alpha to the Omega"

Self-published February 16, 2011 to alphabetically emphasizing short pages on each letter in English alphabet of humans and the attributes of God's perfection.

"MMMA Test Strategy/Guidelines for Aerospace Vehicles"

Published by Martin Marietta Michoud Aerospace, released in April 30, 1986

Covers all technical aspects of design, fabrication and testing for aerospace components through vehicles technically, relevant to that period. Guidelines for Space Station Proposal preparation.

Table of Contents

Introduction

In this world we live in we tend to rely on science and our understanding is that we live in a three-dimensional world. Why do we think that way? Because it is what we can see, touch, examine, etc. We tend not to accept things we cannot touch, see, feel or measure by some accepted standard previously established.

We can see ourselves, the earth, other people, animals and other things, including the sky and universe. The universe becomes more difficult for us as we can see the stars and other planets, solar systems, galaxies, etc. but only understand very little about them. We have examined past life forms in this worlds history and can make educated assumptions about them and why they became extinct. Science has worked on all these types of issues and studied them, but this still just touches the surface about the absolute truth on all of them. Let's face it, Doctors are still finding out more about our human bodies. That's why they call their work practices. Probably all sciences and manmade research and professions should be called practices, as all are still learning and adding to their knowledge databases. Mankind has discovered a lot and understands a lot about all aspects of life and the universe, but still have only touched the surface of absolute facts. I'm not talking about theories and hypothesis, as they are just ideas with some rational to back them up; but are constantly being updated, changed and revised totally at times.

From my own view point, The more I learn the more I see that I don't know or understand, as all new information opens questions on more issues and more unknowns.

This book I hope helps us look at the magnitude of time, space, and how we fit into the overall scheme of things. One serious question is what about the spiritual world, which by itself is a different dimension. Why, because we cannot measure or physically see it. We know it exists or we would not have internal thoughts about it. It is imbedded in our minds and beings. One of the whys and thought processes we cannot totally explain. It does not fit our concept of three-dimensional thought or measurements of science.

Another item we do not totally understand is LOVE or caring for other people, pets, etc. Where does that fit into three-dimensional theory? Likewise, where does Hate fit into all this. If you read my previous books on "A Search for Truth" or "Why Did God Create Us" there are more questions stimulating the big question WHY do we exist (Accident,

God, Evolution, you name it). Additionally, some suggestions of what to do to find the answers.

The Beginning of Thought

Life as we know it starts early in our small little minds and is a continuing adventure to figure everything out. It expands as we grow up and learn more from our surroundings and parents or those taking care of us.

These people have a large influence on our thoughts and ideas which will be constantly changed as we see more of this 3-dimensional world. A lot of it won't make any sense at first but if we are fortunate to have an average or above average IQ, we will start adding it all up and learn more about this world that we see, and why other people are like they are. I'm not talking about race or sex, just other people in this world.

It can be fun trying to understand it all, figuring out how it all fits together and what we like and don't like.

What is life all about and what happens to us when we die?

Life and Existence

As humans we are scientifically trying to figure out everything. It is fun and can be very advantageous to us individually and collectively.

I recall an Electrical Engineer that worked for me in the space program who loved figuring out new things. He did not require much sleep (three to four hours per night), so he worked with us in the Space Program in the day time and went down to Tulane University in the evenings and worked with doctors and scientist who were trying to develop artificial hearts. If we had an unusual problem at work, he would sometimes take the idea home with him and work trying to solve it in a bedroom he had set up like a Laboratory with electronics/Computers/etc.

This life is a lot of fun and working to try to understand everything and solutions to various issues. Problems create a challenging experience. That does 't mean it is easy though. That is true for everyday living, finances, relationships, business, science, religion, God, etc.

We must always study and know history on all issues, science, philosophy, politics, religion, etc. you name it. Why? If we don't we will repeat some of the same mistakes they had in the past.

Our minds and thoughts should always be a work in progress to learn and understand and gain in knowledge and wisdom. That even includes music, sports, you name it. More fun with others who are interested in the same things, even if they have different viewpoints.

This is true even if you are looking at science, religion, the physical world, space, agriculture, oceans, geology, etc. The application and usage of all these are important to our long-range plans and possibilities.

This book is written from a slightly different perspective as it addresses the totality of the universe and what part we play in it or could play in it. Also, is there anything beyond our understanding of the universe. We know very little about our universe, if you can call it ours which is kind of crazy to start with. It does not belong to us.

Per our understanding of science, it's a three-dimensional universe. This is based on what we can see, touch, measure, etc. Just like our world here on earth. One small question? What are the black holes in space that we cannot see stars in? What is in them and does it or will they affect us? This was covered in my previous book from tests performed by using the Hubble Telescope. The results were different then previously thought to be true. The study showed many stars and galaxies moving away from us.

What is important and necessary, etc.? We are just people on a small planet named the earth in a small galaxy called The Milky Way. What else can there be, and can it change over time? More importantly will it affect us or this world now or in the future?

Philosophers have tried to figure it out and came up with various ideas. They usually end up with more why's than real answers. They also do not usually agree totally.

Another question we might ask would be to Medical Doctors or Psychologists. How do we measure or explain thought and thinking? I know they have figured out how to measure brain activity (waves), but not what the person is really thinking or why? We can ask people what they are thinking, but they may or may not respond truthfully, or even understand why they think what they do. We can even use some variation of truth serum, but that only looks at what the person recalls or mentally remembers or knows about the past from their own perspective. What led them to think what they are thinking or how they think or reason things out, that is another question?

Scientifically the aspects and possibilities are larger than life itself.

I have always enjoyed debating these type issues as well as other issues such as: Why are we here, how did it all begin, purpose for our existence, differences throughout our world, people, species, and all different variables we do not totally understand.

Religiously speaking we could ask Drs. of Theology about how they know if a person has accepted that there is a God or something beyond our own existence. This was covered in detail in my previous books. For the purposes of this book I will just stipulate my own thoughts and relate it to the first Chapter of Romans in The Holy Bible. Since the very beginning of time as we know it, mankind has recognized there is something beyond us and this world and tried to understand it. Then try to make up their own ideas about it, or they may choose to run away from those thoughts. Many people are uncomfortable or avoid it all together; thus, limit themselves to what we can see, touch and feel, or some variations of these measurable things in life. Others have made up their own ideas (gods, statues, concepts, etc. up to and including atheism {there is nothing else}). If we can't see it or measure it, then does it exist. That is why so many try to explain it in physical terms (statues, the moon, an outer space rock, etc.). No one can totally know what someone else has decided or know all the answers.

As we learn more from the various sciences, the world has changed a lot overtime and so has the universe. Physically we live in a three-dimensional world, but is there a fourth or fifth dimension? Space, Time, etc. themselves can be fun to try to figure out. Almost all we discover or come up with was already here and we are just starting to figure some of it out. It is a very complex world we live in. It even gets harder when you start talking or investigating the Universe, Space, a Spiritual Dimension, etc.

I don't pretend to know all the answers and believe anyone who thinks they do understand any subject totally is extremely egotistical. We keep learning more in every field of science, physical, medically, emotionally, DNA, religion, you name it. Our existence and world are far beyond our total understanding and perceptions. We are still in our infancy in understanding everything. Many people in the world yesterday and today are just trying to survive, let alone think or study the totality of it all.

One simple question demonstrates our continual learning process and inadequacy to explain it all. How big is big and how small is small? In the recent past, even that has changed overtime. The universe keeps getting bigger as demonstrated in our research of space and galaxies/stars. We used to think the atom was the smallest thing, but now science has gone to various size of atoms (types) down to even the sizes of particles that make up the atoms.

This book as titled is looking at our three-dimensional universe and other potential dimensions. These obviously exist in my opinion, beyond our three-dimensional universe. The fun part is we collectively know very little about other dimensions.

Our Thinking Processes and Dimensions

Dimensions are not normally thought about much today. We tend to think in Height, Width, Depth, Time, Distances and things we can see and measure by some method. That could be physically or electronically in our modern age. All the many various ways we can measure anything. Many people are amazed at how we are now influenced by digital, Computer Systems, I Phones, IPADs, the internet, etc. Many use them but do not comprehend how they work. Even children use them for games, and in High School for class work now days that change our thinking, planning and how we even look at the world. Our world keeps expanding into new areas and capabilities, but still only touches the surface of the totality of all that is possible.

Our selfish or self-centered ways are sort of common to mankind.

It is like Adam and Eve wanting and being tempted to have more of everything. They listened to Satan (the serpent) that tempted them away from God's directions, wisdom and perfect world. How you might ask? It is simple; they wanted more knowledge and to be able to do whatever they wanted to do.

How could that happen? Simple. Our minds limited dimensional thought process and free will thought makes us think it all might be better: and we are willing to take that chance for something better. A little like gambling trying to get something more. We will all do some of that as it is built into our selfish, free will mind set.

Another thing that gets us into trouble is alcohol or drugs. Why, to get away from our problems or relax from our attempt at controlling our own circumstances. Sometimes just to have more fun or gain more wealth, power, you name it, but they can all backfire on us.

All of these come from mental thoughts, free will and trying to control our own destiny. Thoughts are a form of dimensional thinking we don't totally understand but can be controlled.

In general, we don't really think much about how we think or reason. Nor do we think much about things outside our life expectances, such as light years, eternal life, etc. With age and seeing family and friends die it gives us a slightly different perspective and thought process. We do think about why there is illness, hardships, our physical health and maybe history, governments, life expectancy, finances, family and things like sports, sewing, reading, cooking, deserts, etc. Even some of those are passing away from our thoughts as we have become consumer oriented, not makers or repair oriented. Just remove and replace it with the latest thing or something perceived to be better. Some of that can be fun if we are doing it with others who enjoy the same things, such as sports, science, music, reading novels, or history, religion, etc. you name it.

The question is what happens to you at death and where do you go, or do you just get buried and that's it? If we think we exist after death, why, and where do we go, or which path do we take?

These are thoughts outside our measurable dimensions and normal worldly thought processes; but our thoughts and minds wonder about it and these other dimensions, or concepts if you will at times.

From here let us look at some dimensional thought processes beyond our physical known world.

Biblically, one day Satan and his demons, and all non-believers in Christ will be destroyed and sent to Hell. Another Dimension we do not want to be a part of. Me'ism or me first gets us going that direction.

On the other hand, God's love and forgiving Grace through His son provide us a route to an eternal life in Heaven as God's children.

Big choice for us - just like Adam and Eve had in The Holy Bible (all versions).

Our Perception of
Other Dimensions

Scientifically and philosophically most of
what we read or study deals with one living,
breathing earthly existence. Why? Because
that is what we can see and directly affects
our life here on earth, that we think we can
at least generally understand.

All science and our physical world that we can identify with is this physical world that is measurable and quantifiable to some respect. It may be very small or very large, but still fits into our measurable concept. Mentally we are aware there is more, but have difficulty getting our arms and minds around them. All people of this world can identify with the idea that there is more that we don't understand, but obviously the world, creation if you will, is beyond our total comprehension.

Science Fiction and Philosophy has continually come up with and added ideas. There have been many religions that attack or try to define these other dimensions. They have developed ideas of other planets, different types of gods and even killed others to defend their ideas and concepts. Some have created Deities of stone, individual people (Rulers, Kings, etc.), volcanos, animals, the Sun and the Moon, etc., etc.

The real question is what is beyond our Three-Dimensional world. Who is in control, plus what happens when it is over or our physical lives end?

If God created the Universe and all that exists then He is beyond our three-dimensional world. The Spiritual world is not "Measurable" or "Dimensional" in our terms. It therefore is beyond our total comprehension.

The Trinity in Gen 1:26-31 discussed it and they decided to create mankind in their image and likeness. That would imply we have a physical body, mind and body like Christ and a spiritual nature like God and the Holy Spirit. Therefore, we have a spiritual nature beyond our science and worldly understanding of dimensions.

The question then is how we relate to this spiritual world, which is outside our physical dimensions and ideas.

We don't totally understand our three-dimensional world, let alone the spiritual dimension.

I chose to call this the Spiritual Dimension as it is our Lord's and our Spiritual being. I rule out Atheism as it believes in nothing except this world that arrived accidently, and we are all just smart primates that will eventually die.

Most religions other than Christianity do not have realistic futures, and a loving caring God that provides a long-term future beyond physical death or at best unrealistic afterlife ideas. Some even propose becoming a different animal or a pecking order of does and don'ts to acquire an afterlife or a continuation of life that is beyond belief in our simple minds. They even classify sexes (male, female, and classes of people/race to be at different levels in the pecking order).

This is obviously ridiculously wrong as there are and have been great people and intellects in all races and sexes in this world.

It should be noted here that God put us in charge of this world He created to take care of it, not destroy it. It is all His, but we are to husband it (Care for it) {Reference first part of Genesis}.

Who is this God or Creator or are we just an accident? Did we just get lucky that this planet we call earth has an environment and living creatures and a climate that supports life as we know it? Don't think so!

This book addresses issues like my previous books but from a different perspective. For this reason, they touch on an understanding or acceptance of the fact that there is an unknown dimension that we may never totally understand or completely know. Why do I say that is simple? We will never have the capacity to understand totally all of God's Dimension and wisdom! We must just accept Him and continue to search ways to understand His ways and what He wants of us. Then serve Him as number one in our lives and then serve others as He would want us to do.

He is all knowing and encompasses everything. He has total/all knowledge, and is always, present (Omnipotent, Omnipresent, etc.).

God's Total Reality and Dimension

Tough to talk about unless you believe there is more to life/existence than just this world and our physical life (Dimension/reality if you will).

There appears to be two added dimensions, but one is under the other. One is evil and operated by Satan and his demons and the larger one which is over it all is God's Dimension. We are caught between the two. In one we are sinners that puts us in Satan's zone/dimension. The other is God's dimension which is over everything. With God's Love and Grace, we can move into His dimension by accepting Him, Loving and Honoring Him with our total beings and then Serving Him with the aid of The Holy Spirit. Reference Hebrews 11 and 12 which defines how mankind original became part of God's plan/ kingdom: i.e. Righteous enough to be His. Basically, through Faith/belief in Him and following Him.

I remember a man coming to our church in Metairie, La. that represented The Gideons

(The Holy Bible Distributors to hospitals, Hotels, motels, etc.). He would always give a presentation on what functions they performed and then give a talk illustrating our common human problem. We are constantly bombarded by three entities: our own selfishness, Satan trying to lead us the wrong direction as he is the Great Deceiver and The Holy Spirit talking to us to lead us in God's way, truth and life.

He would use one hand to represent Satan and one to represent God. Each hand would be on each side of our heads by our ears trying to talk to us and lead us their direction. We of course were in the middle and had to choose which way to follow or go.

Biblically speaking, one day Satan's power and presence will be destroyed, and he and his demons will be sent to Hell along with all non-believers in our Lord and Savior, Jesus The Christ. That is throughout the scriptures.

Our problem is our own self-centeredness or "me'ism" which we must over come with God's help, Grace, Love and sacrificial gift of His Son's perfect life and sacrifice.

God gave us free will to choose which way we would go. Choose a loving God who has an eternal plan for us in Heaven, or damnation in Hell.

One idea I came up with to control my thoughts is a very simple explanation how we can improve ourselves. I at the time was in the USAF and most people in the service used a lot of profanity. Having been a teacher in electronics, computers and radar systems I decided our mind works like a computer.

That led me to think I could stop using or even thinking about profanity. Mentally if I heard or even thought of one, I would amplify it in my mind to stop me from using them or saying them. It surprisingly worked extremely well.

Later, I started interrupting others if they used the Lord, God, Jesus, etc. in vain or in properly. I would simply say "He had nothing to do with it". They would usually stop and respond, "who had nothing to do with it". It made them stop and think or at least acknowledge they did not even know why they used God, etc. name. At least they quit using them around me.

My point is with The Holy Spirits help and our conscience thought process and actions we can improve our thoughts, speaking and way of addressing issues in our lives. We could also help others do the same. This will obviously help our families, children and friends be better people mentally and spiritually.

God's Dimension

If we accept the fact that God exists and that The Holy Bible is our aide along with His Holy Spirit. Then use it to help us through this life and prepare us for the next phase or dimension of our existence. Then we are on the right track, but it will always be difficult for us to accept it all. God's total capabilities and eternal existence, i.e. His dimension is so far greater than anything we can comprehend or understand. We just must accept that He exists and is The Creator of it all and has a plan for us that covers eternity. **He is Love and literally the Light of this world and our existence**. If you recall from my previous book "Why Did God Create Us", we are mere ants on a small planet in a small Galaxy that He created. Still difficult to understand or accept it all, but we must if we are going to be a part of His overall plan. Reference Hebrews 11, especially Hebrews 11:6, We must first accept that He exists and second seek to find and know Him then thirdly serve Him and He will reward us. Consider reading all of Hebrews 11 and 12. What is Righteousness and how do we acquire it: FAITH THAT HE EXIST AND FOLLOW HIM TOTALLY BY FAITH AND TRUST!

Then there is that big Question - WHY? Why do bad things happen to good people, etc.? Why are some born under terrible circumstances or have terrible things happen to them? My only response is that this world is evil and has been contaminated by Satan and all our self-centered, me first thinking. God created perfection and Satan and our me'ism contaminated it.

He is The Creator and the Originator of the plan and how to overcome the evil that Satan and his fallen angels and our own me'ism (our self-centered thought processes) has jeopardized that plan. He is number one and the master of everything, but still created us, loves us and provided Jesus as our way into His kingdom and Glory through His loving Grace offering. He came to save us from damnation by being a perfect human to serve as our one and only perfect sacrifice and then took our place on the cross followed by His resurrection and returned to Father God.

God's love is beyond dimensions and He is over all dimensions. So, let us get straight with Our God and Redeemer. Just thank You for leaving us The Holy Spirit and The Word to help-us find The Way, The Truth and The Life You promised us.

Why oh Why do we exist, birds fly, fish swim, the earth, space and universe exist? Why does time exist, and we exist during part of it?

Note: He is beyond TIME as we know it and unlimited (The Alpha and Omega, The Beginning and the End, or otherwise from minus infinity to plus infinit)

How can I say all this?

1. The Trinity (Father God, The Son, and The Holy Spirit) decided to create us in His image. That means Physically, Mentally, Body, Mind and Spirit, See Genesis 1: 26-31). Why, I believe He wanted to share His Love

and Kingdom to those who would willingly accept Him and His plan of salvation. Maybe He wanted to replace all the angels that were thrown out of heaven with Satan that thought they were better than God and wanted their own way. I can't totally answer that, as I am too insignificant and just a human being with the limitations associated with that. But as He stated in Matthew 17:20 "If you have the faith of a mustard seed you can move Mountains". There are those words again Our Faith and His Grace.

2. Tough to swallow all that unless you believe and accept God is everywhere present and can do anything except sin, be evil or be unholy!

3. If there is no spiritual or Godly dimension then we live and die the best we can, period! No Hope or future period!

4. **Where do we or humanity go with these concepts?**

Letting God's Dimension Lead Us

In my terminology God's Dimension can only lead us one way — His Way.

The Holy Spirit is with us to help us by leading us to God and accepting our Lord and Savior Jesus Christ. He then is here to help us study and learn more about the Trinity and how to serve God and others (remember Matthew 28: 18- 20). First, we must believe He exists and seek Him out (Hebrews 11:6). If we accept The Lord Jesus the Christ we will be saved eternally and then want to serve Him the rest of our lives, following His Word The Holy Bible and His Spirits leading. His reward is eternal life with the Trinity and all believers.

Jesus provided The Way, The Truth and The Life Everlasting. The Way is straight forward as Christ was the perfect example and His prayer of obedience in the Garden before His crucifixion - "Not My Will Father (God the Father), but Thy Will Be Done".

One pastor I had for many years used to have winter bible studies for the first month or so of the year. He had his Dr. of Theology Degree and had been a Seminary Professor for several years. As he went through a study of a book in the Bible he would cover each verse of the scripture in that book. He frequently would stop on a potentially controversial verse or scriptures and present the various theological positions on that scripture/topic. He would then explain the basis of each position and then why he believed one position was what he believed to be the correct theological correct view. He never suggested you accept his position. I never had a problem with his position as I believed his view agreed with mine or I adapted to the better view, but usually already agreed with his view. I believe he and I were following what the Holy Spirit was directing us to think. I loved it.

I have had other Theologians I did not agree with, but at least could understand where they were coming from. Usually with only minor variations that did not miss the major points of the scripture.

We are always to be studying His Word "The Holy Bible" and in my case I have read a scripture/passage many times and each time grow a deeper insight and understanding, without changing the original basic idea, just adding to it.

Always adding to not taking anything away. I believe this was because The Holy Spirit was leading me. Maturity in any field of study comes from studying and applying what we learn. Studying can be by reading, working, or implementing the ideas.

I dare you to take a Book in The Holy Bible, read it and study it then go back some time later after applying it and see if you don't grow from it and better understand it.

My Personnal Lazarus Story

This is not meant to take away from what Christ did with Lazarus, just an example of God's greatness in my life and family. I know it helped a neighbor and his wife get back to church together. They were from different religious denominations and sort of had been drifting

Others that knew what happened to me became more active, not because of me but because of the Grace of God. I believe He had more for me to do for Him and others or I would not be here.

<u>I believe every human has been placed here to fulfill God's plan and has a gift or gifts to perform that purpose. What is his plan for you?</u>

To start my personal story, I will walk you through some of my life, including what I will call my Lazarus occurrence.

I was always a very active person at work, schooling, with family and play as some of which you can see in my "Background" write up. I will therefore skip some of that information or at least try not to repeat it.

I started noticing when I was out doing yard work that I would frequently have to stop and take a break. Get a cold drink and sit down for a few minutes. I would then proceed and finish the yard work. It seemed to be occurring more and more frequently. I had always been a very active person with sports and doing my own yard and repair work around the house. I just figured I was just getting older and needed to take it a little easier with breaks as required.

My wife and I both had artificial knees by this time and she had had seven fusions in her back. She also had had three heart bypasses. Anyway, I decided that I would talk to her Cardiologist the next time we went in for her checkup. He gave me an EKG which was fine but suggested further testing.

After the tests, he came in and told me I was a walking dead man. I had 5 heart arteries that were 80, 90, & 100% blocked. Obviously, I needed bypass surgery, which we had done. I was now in my 70s.

All went well, and I was back keeping busy again at my normal activity at church, with family, golf, etc.

The next part of my story is not written from my knowledge but from the family and medical records, because I don't remember any of it.

I know the results but not the details.

Back to the unusual, I call a God experience.

In June 2013, we had taken a trip up to Little Rock, Arkansas with my Daughter's family to see a new Great Grand Baby (Irie Gold McManus). While there one evening we went down a few blocks from their home to have supper and on the way back the granddaughter, her husband, the baby and I walked back while the rest drove back. As we were walking along I fell over on the side walk dead at 76 years old.

Two female Doctors (one had just graduated) ran over from opposite sides of street and started CPR on me. A police car at the end of the block called for an ambulance and two prayer groups were started on each side of the street. When the ambulance arrived, they shocked me at least twice to try and to get my heart started again and took me to the University of Arkansas Medical Hospital.

At the hospital they started me on a new procedure of putting me into an Ice Coma and I'm sure other things which I'm not aware of to try to save my life. The procedures they performed I understand were not even available in the state of Louisiana at that time.

The doctors told the family they did not know whether I would live or die or if I would be mentally functional afterword. I was in the hospital from June13 to 25th of 2013, After some time, I started to come around and they inserted a defibrillator in my chest, which would shock my heart if it ever stopped again. I do not remember the trip up to Arkansas and the next few weeks, except for stories the family told me about.

I believe God was not through with me yet, so he guided Doctors and whole procedure to save my life back to my same old self.

After recovery period I was back doing the things he had me doing before and it is why I believe I started writing these books to try and reach others for Him. My first book "A Search for Truth" was started in various pieces years ago and I thought it would be mainly for family and churches. Of course, it is not about me, but about the Trinity of God leading others, I'm just his servant helping to spread the word for hopefully His harvest of those who will accept Him as Lord.

Why He chose me I have no idea, except that I already was His. Happy to serve Him in any capacity. I am now going on 82 and still serving my Lord and Master. I was back in choirs, serving as a deacon, witnessing and playing golf again.

My Thought Process and Foundation

My conclusion and firm foundation and belief is best represented by a Psalm of praise and adoration. This Psalm/Song wraps up my thought process on the Unknown Dimension that I know exists and is part of my very being.

The following is a Biblical (Psalm) on the subject at hand, which is paraphrased into my words using Psalms 8 from The Holy Bible (NIV) to match the subject of this book.

When I look into the night sky and see your work; the moon, stars and all that is suspended in space.

What are we mere Humans that You are mindful of us.

You have allowed us mere humans that believe in you and serve you a crown of glory and honor and have made us to be a little lower than the angels.

You have allowed us to be in charge of all this worlds creation: The beasts of the field, The birds of the air, The fish of the sea.

But what are we that You are mindful of Us.

O Lord our God the majesty and glory of Your name transcends the earth and fills the heavens and always will!

O Lord our God all your children praise You perfectly, to your Honor and Glory Forever and ever, Amen!

Everything should give you all the Glory and Majesty of Your Name, let alone Your very Eternal Being and Greatness!

God's dimension is so far above us and beyond us we can only praise Him and The Majesty and Glory of Your Name, realizing that He is beyond this universe and dimension as He created it all.

God's dimension is so far above us and beyond us we can only praise Him and realize that He is beyond this universe and dimension as He created it all.

Never try to put Him in a box that fits your finite mind or thought processes as He is so far beyond us we will never

<u>in this life time totally understand Him and probably never will in totality as we are just part of His creation and He loves us.</u>

Mankind and religions have always attempted to do that, which is absurd to even consider. He is GOD the all-knowing Holy One who created it all.

If we accept and believe in You and Your sacrificial gift of love and forgiveness provided through The Trinity (Father, Son and Holy Spirit), we one day will become totally part of **Your eternal family and are permanently changed from this sinful world.**

Your Son as part of the Trinity came out of heaven as a mere baby served and showed us "The Way, The Truth and The Life". He served the perfect life, to be the perfect Sacrificial Lamb to save us all, if we just believe and follow His example and serve. We were provided the Holy Spirit to council, teach and direct our path. What a wonderful Loving God we have!

We are sealed to His family when we believe this in our heart, mind and soul, and then share that belief with others (ref. **Romans 10:9,10**). Also, reference **Ephesians 1: 9** that when we totally accept Christ Jesus sacrificial death and resurrection the Holy Spirit seals us into God's Family and we are to serve God's plans for us. This entity is part of the Trinity "The Holy Spirit". The Holy Bible clarifies all this for us, but we must trust Him and study it and develop trust in His guidance with the aid of His Spirit showing us the truths. We become part of His Kingdom and family forever, but it is hard to make that first huge step.

Our job, if you will, is to serve Him here and now and become more what He wants us to be (Sanctified). That is the process of maturing to be more like He wants us to be. Won't be completed until we go to be with Him after our physical life ends. It is called the Sanctification Process, which should be part of our Christian maturing to become more like he wants us to be.

God loved us before we even existed outside the womb. He sacrificed His only begotten Son (Jesus the Christ) to provide The Word and The Way and Life, before we existed. He left Glory in Heaven as part of the Trinity, came to earth as a baby and lived a perfect sinless life so He could be the perfect sacrifice for our sins. Hard to imagine His sacrificial love, leaving God's Holy perfect dimension in Heaven and coming down here as a baby and living a perfect life and death for us mere humans. He arouse from the grave and returned to the Father in Heaven to show us the way for us. He did not leave us without a powerful counselor, helper, and adviser who also sealed us into God's Family once we accepted Him and willingly share this great news to the world we live in.

Thank You for Your Holy Spirit's presences in our life as believers forever.

The following is one example of my continual thoughts and a medley of three songs.

"His Grace Never Leaves Me and Keeps Me Singing as I Go"

The following is the combined music (words) of "Amazing Grace," "No Never Alone," and "He Keeps Me Singing," which I consolidated back in 1980s. They tell a story that puts it all together for me and my thought process, beliefs, and what I look forward to:

"Amazing grace! How sweet the sound, that saved a wretch like me! I once was lost but now am found, was blind, but now I see. I've seen the lightning flashing and heard the thunder roll, I've felt sin's breakers dashing, trying to conquer my soul: I've heard the voice of Jesus, telling me still to fight on, He promised never to leave me, never to leave me alone. And because of this promise There's within my heart a melody, Jesus whispers sweet and low: Fear not, I am with thee, peace, be still, in all life's ebb and flow. Jesus, Jesus, Jesus, sweetest name I know, Fills my every longing, keeps me singing as I go. T'was grace that taught my heart to fear, and grace my fears relieved; How precious did that grace appear, the hour I first believed! The world's fierce winds are blowing; temptations are sharp and keen; I feel a peace in knowing, my Savior stands between; He stands to shield me from danger, when earthly friends are gone, He promised never to leave me, never to leave me alone. All my life was wrecked by sin and strife, discord filled my heart with pain, Jesus swept across the broken strings, stirred the slumbering chords again. Jesus, Jesus, Jesus, sweetest name I know, Fills my every longing, keeps me singing as I go. Thro' many dangers, toils, and snares, I have already come, My Savior helps me to carry, my cross when heavy to bear, My feet entangled with briars, ready to cast me down; My Savior whispers His promise, never to leave me alone. No, never alone, no, never alone, He promised never to leave me, never to leave me alone. Though sometimes He leads through waters deep, Trials fall across my way, Though sometimes the path seems rough and steep, His footprints lead all the way: Jesus, Jesus, Jesus, sweetest name I know, Fills my every longing, keeps me singing as I go. When we have been there ten thousand years, bright shining as the sun, We've no less days to sing God's praise than when we first begun. He died for me on the mountain, for me they pierced His side, For me He opened the fountain, of crimson, cleansing blood; For me He waiteth in glory, seated upon

His throne; He promised never to leave me, never to leave me alone. Soon He is coming back to welcome me, far beyond the starry sky; I shall wing my flight to worlds unknown; I shall reign with Him on high. Jesus, Jesus, Jesus, sweetest name I know, Fills my every longing, keeps me singing as I go."

"Acknowledgements"

To all the many family members, teachers, ministers, friends and especially God's guidance by The Holy Spirit and The Holy Bible.

My wife and son who helped edit this writing and loved the approach and thought process.

Too many to list and some I probably don't even remember from my younger years.

Of course, The Holy Bible which I have read numerous times and given lessons on for years to different classes and shared with family, friends and employees that worked for me in the Aerospace Program, when appropriate. When they wanted to learn or know more about where I was coming from or what I might understand about God. We must always be learning and studying His Word and directions as we will never know it all. He is so far beyond our minds and capabilities. We as His children are to share The Good News, Matthew 28:18-20.

Also, reference my previous books "A Search For Truth" and "Why Did God Create Us", but mainly study the Holy Bible.

All references in this book besides The Holy Bible use mostly information about individuals that I knew or had worked for me, music and specific biblical passages. All I believe I was being lead by The Holy Spirit to use in my writings.

About the Author

Ray was born Raymond E. Weaver to Christian parents in Kansas City, Missouri in 1936. He had a sister and a brother 9 ½ and 6 ½ years older than him respectively. Ray accepted Christ as his Savior at 10 years old and was baptized. He has attempted to study the Holy Bible and follow God ever since with some usual difficulties growing up in his youth, and has rededicated his life many times since, with no doubts about initially accepting the Lord and being led by Him throughout life. Ray has been a High School Bible Class Department Leader for approximately 10 years and taught both couples classes and men's classes for over 35 years and a Deacon for 20 plus years. He also has played Cornet in a Church Orchestra for a few years and has been in choirs for probably close to 45 years.

Both parents were born before 1900 (1891 & 1899 respectively), and both had tough lives from early ages. His father lost his father when he was killed in 1899 while they were homesteading in the Oklahoma Territory. Ray's mother after 7 years old, lived in other people's houses taking care of their elderly parents and grandparents.

We lost our Grandson in law to a jet ski and boating accident while still in his 20's. A great Christian man who was considering going into ministry, and their second baby on the way that he did not even know about. So many variations in this world with children born in poverty, etc. All this helped me question or ask why all these variations, life styles, circumstances for people exist and bad things happen to good people (See Chapter 6 for answer).

I have no doubts about initially accepting the Lord and being led by Him throughout life.

Ray's father worked his way through to a Doctors Degree in Optometry and watch and clock repair schooling. He also was wounded in the Army during WW1. He developed, owned, and operated a Jewelry Story in K.C., Mo. for 40 + years. Ray's mother worked her way through what was then called Business College. They were married at 30 and 22 years old respectively. There were not any government assistance programs then, you had to work hard at whatever you could and drive forward, no freebees, or assistance, period.

Some of Ray's ancestry in this country goes back before the Revolutionary War to 1660 or earlier and all his ancestry were from Europe (Irish, German, English, French, etc.).

After High School at 17, Ray started college at William Jewel College in Liberty, Mo with a major in Theology and a minor in Music. He had won the Aeron Award in Music in High School as a Trumpet/Cornet player and Librarian of the music library, which was the largest in K.C., Mo. except for the Kansas City Symphony Orchestra. He also lettered in Football. Ray also learned to fix watches and clocks as a teenager at his father's jewelry store (Weavers Jewelry) in Kansas City, Missouri.

Ray and his Wife of 63 years were married, in Denver, Colorado and now have 2 children and spouses, 6 grandchildren and 7 great grandchildren. All of them and respective spouses and children that are old enough are believers in our Lord Jesus Christ.

Ray stopped college and went into the USAF during the end of the Korean War, where he studied and taught Electronics, Computers and Radar Systems at Lowry AF Base in Denver. He and his wife were married in Denver and while in the USAF and had two children. He transferred to Ladd AF Base in Fairbanks, Alaska in 1957 (before it was a state). He worked in laboratory and flight line work on the F89J fighter Interceptors as part of the USAF Defense Command.

After leaving the AF in March of 1959 he went to work for The Boeing Co. in Wichita, Kansas, working on the ASG-15 Fire Control

Systems (Radar & Control Systems) on the new B52G Bombers. He also returned to college at the University of Wichita with a major in Physics. He later transferred to Seattle, Wash. to work testing the new Bomarc Pilotless Interceptors and returned to college at the University of Washington continuing his work on a Physics degree.

He later transferred to Hill AF Base in Ogden, Utah to develop testing for the Minuteman Missile (ICBMs) and attending the Univ. of Utah studying Physics. This was followed with a transfer to New Orleans area to work on the S-1C First Stage of the Apollo Moon Rocket at NASA's Michoud Assembly and Test Facility in 1964. He now was also attending LSUNO (now known as UNO) working toward a management degree. He was supervising Test Engineering Laboratories performing Development, Qualification, and Reliability Test on S-1C components and systems during this time and managed a Test Engineering Area, electronic assembly and test areas until December 1973.

After 15 years with Boeing, he transferred his work to Martin Marietta Aerospace still at the Michoud NASA Facility developing and testing the External Tanks (ETs) for the Space Shuttle starting in January 1974. He retired from then Lockheed Martin Corp in 2001 at 65 years old) having completed 28 years with LMC (MMC and Lockheed had a merger in 1996). His last major assignment was overseeing the Test Engineering part of the Space Station Proposal Team as a Senior Engineering Manager. Almost all his working career was involved in Test Engineering, with some time over Tool Design, Manufacturing and Manufacturing Process (Manufacturing Engineering).

CPSIA information can be obtained
at www.ICGtesting.com
Printed in the USA
BVHW031540140119
537802BV00003B/11/P

9 781973 647850